THE NOISE OF THE FIELDS

HUGH MAXTON

The Noise of the Fields

POEMS 1970-1975

THE DOLMEN PRESS

*Set in Baskerville type and printed and published in the
Republic of Ireland at the Dolmen Press, North Richmond Street,
Dublin 1.*

First published 1976

ISBN *0 85105 294 0*

*This book is the Summer 1976 Choice
of the Poetry Book Society*

*General distributors in the U.S.A. and in Canada
Humanities Press Inc.
171 First Avenue
Atlantic Highlands
NJ 07716, U.S.A.*

FOR SHEELAGH

CONTENTS

A BLANK MAP

I

You cannot reach the village
or come anywhere near it.
Eternally it retreats

through an elaborate quadrille
of thorns and honeysuckle.
Missionaries find its welcome

hostile, its lust for faith almost
a desire to corrupt. And when
their thoughts turn again to home

the countryside becomes
suddenly impenetrable:
the road inclines, but signposts lie;

caught in a habit of imprecision
they are half destroyed by rust
or glimmer in heat double-miraged.

The image cannot be trusted;
no country has been so badly blessed.

II

There was a rumour of Gaelic
spoken here last week; a cousin
surprised it in a sepia pub.

No one believes the faculty
of speech has survived
Synge's camera: his sheep

9

laze at the foot of a man
thin as the switch he carries.
Perhaps he is the one Parnell

whipped in retelling the story
from Avondale to Aughrim mill.
All this recurs outside

Morgan Mackey's public house
on a granite step as smooth
as hair, brown as a photograph

and scanty as language.

III

Renewing years outside the store.
Fifty-two buses caught in a year
revv again in the instant

and explode like musketry.
There are ramparts of beech around
the barracks, these the sole signs

of order. Elsewhere which is here
walls crumble, slates collapse.
We have thrown bicycles against a gable

built for the firing squad
at Laragh and Drumgoff, symbol
of *imperium* lost now

a broken bottle in the trees.
Three narrow doors stare at us
in the absence of ground floor windows:

it were easier for a rebel
to see Heaven than walk out one of these.

IV

The metally whirring displays
the whiteness of water and air
together, blank when each is alone,

sibling elements of the universe
and only children of a seeming mind
— of a sudden all rots like ash

or becomes blurred glass, sand-blinded.
(Memory's mutual sepsis chose
this moment for my road

back to a jubilee saucer
smeared with Woodbines or
tobacco dottles, an inheritance.)

The Leyland shakes on rubber tyres
as the Square fills with shivvering
columns of diesel and tarfumes;

the chassis trembles. I see cheeks
of my grandparent shake at death
to no avail. There is a hiss

of released brakes and bodywork
as she moves forward away from me.

V

No matter how brackish the stream
or how swollen in flood, water
where it turns is pure silver;

to be unchanging and never the same
the stone's dullness swims
brilliantly where light parks.

There let our eyes find rest
and the water turn turtle, bits of it
becoming airborne.

As we lie dressing by the stream
two dragonflies of unusual blue
pass their lives above our heads.

Our limbs have measured this lasting place;
when we stand up to leave
different water winks

between the crenellated trees.
Soft grass has flayed us while we slept.

VIEWS

I

A cataract of ivy
blinds the bridge's eye;

slow as a crocodile
rust eats the weirwheels.

II

Night arranges its paws about the city,
settles down tired to sleep.

The teeth of a thousand apartments
are dulled,

eyes battened down
against the dawn.

III

Illusion and reality,
growing grasses and stone
were fused near Andechs
and two places seemed one.

Nostalgia's there and now
spoke of a hidden spring,
flourishing acanthus
beneath the lichen.

DOWTH

The hazel and the blackthorn
may contend on the barrow,
the soft wood and the hard wood
locked in dialogue,
but the actual cattle
graze onwards in the meadow.

Pictures create more than they possess
containing within our lines and contours
more than the momentary thing;
just as the dead who scratched their orders
on lintel and capstone
still press our fingers to their lips.

The dead behind the frame alter.
And the memory of a middle-aged poet
with her stockings wrinkled
in an open cemetery
shifts gradually in perspective
out of such mere focus.

Coming then to the site of some
irreparable intrusion on nature
we are impressed not so much
by the durability of stone
but the absence of Lord Netterville's teahouse,
which used to dominate the scene.

1968

SLIGO

The terrace has made way
for the shifting scree;

the scorched hill absorbs
whatever little springs
from the remote stones;

the coarse grass
and saltsmitten weeds
hide the luminous land.

I have stood with you here
listening to the harsh briars
and the loss of this wilderness,

barren, soundless
like the pause in some elegy.

RISK
i. m. Máirtín Ó Cadhain

When you chaired a meeting in Trinity
you refused to open until the man
from the Special Branch had left the back row.
You sat there reading while the audience
hoped you weren't making a fool of yourself.
At last someone deserted out of loyalty.

We never saw you as a widower
vainly stocking a life with whiskey,
nor saw the massive verso timetables
which you wrote those last stories on, nor heard
your shy inquiries about drainage maps.
The Sheaves are Stacked; your shade is lightening now.

At the funeral you scored a final point,
refusing to hear a volley of shots.

THE LOUGH

No ships are sailing the Foyle; look at them;
here is a sense of vanished water.
The wharves are tubes of pulpy wood
standing in water. Will they relieve
the sieges that we have known? Booms across
the mind echo deadly over water.

A copse we would call the trees at Culmore
but for permanent smoke from passing trains,
ghosting earlier freights. The countryside
thrives on our exhausted breath and rinses it.
We have no need to look at each other
or complain of chimneys in the landscape.

In the heart of the humble clouds there is
the ever-bright flame of waste oxygen.

PREMONITION OF WINTER

We have come to love this coastline. Clearly
the cobbles here are looser than in town
and the dust is crystalline. We nearly
think another world begins or, grown
casual, imagine seas and channels
separate us from the work-a-day mass.

But these rocks are the more ancient hells,
the acid coves and strands of powdered glass.
In Antrim sheep were bled white by a beast
not known to man but intimate with gland
and artery. A whale skidded at least
twelve yards ashore against the rush of land.

In the town they talk of peace and justice
and have never known the sea turn to ice.

DE PROFUNDIS

The fossil-fish is pale; we mined this pair
just forty minutes out from the hotel.
We thought it deader than the dinosaur,
a pattern in stone, an empty cell-
ular abstraction. Which proved an error.
Below the dreaming tropic lies a chill
region flattened by thirty gravities;
and water there is thicker than blood,
small and lucid as a lens which is
the sum of what it sees. History's rude
moralities are rammed down on us,
the teething beasts that we live among.

We rise with bursting bodies and confound
the placid statisticians on the ground.

THE CAUSEWAY

We crossed the shaking river about five,
a plume of smoke tossing on the city,
our engines running docile as heifers
through wet pastures flowing though level.

The countryside suffers from perfection.
Immaculate anonymous births
walk their witness into the earth.
The soil winces under their even feet.

We are princes whose father is no king
but wear a master's face. Throughout his death
the dogs stand trembling, fat cattle tremble.
For once all moves to the metronome's shocks.
To-night we sleep on the east coast beneath
a causeway that hides the chattering rocks.

COUSIN

He will come back to the same county,
a house which snuggled round our soft bones,
a silent garden where flowers stood at ease;
as cousins we lived in that playground of air.

Younger than he was, we grew up faster
and turned the land over for a purpose.
He comes back to the same house, trusting
in some hidden moment in our past;
but the road is widened and unfamiliar,
its blue ribs greased and even. The trees
he hid in are still wet, but are illegible;
the noise of the fields a drunken language.

Standing weakly by the painted house
the ghost of an only child sips at his tears.

•ODE

To read our few poets
you'd think there had been
a recent withdrawal
from the land of the stoat
and the yellow-scarf mouse;

a land in which nothing
twitches in the woodlands
but our nerves,
and every swan
is someone else's daughter.

Their lives are mashed
in the engine of politics
or, high on dynamite,
they industrialise the old dreads.
Yet truth is

ours is still a rural country.
In which we never need
the stoat for savagery
or the yellow-scarf
for extinction.

NOCTURNE

Night on the accustomed
roadway draws past;
commercial mottoes
hidden in its plush,

ancestral fragments
launched on the lost
kinetic fears
the hours conjure.

Tiny instances of war
sound alone,
and the barometer
draws itself upright.

In the morning
the usual rubbish
falls from my bowels;
I smell of my father.

OBSERVATORY GARDENS W. 8
for Sheelagh in Derry

Silence in the gathered city;
the sky a shell drawn down to hear;
black air nudges at the window
defining the calm loneliness

of a new urban man. When I arrived
yesterday, misquoting Empson,
my host gently reproved me
in the tone of the master himself.

(Remember before we were married
I told you about his reading
and proud reference to
arthritis of the upper lip?)

Now once more I am hushed
and surrounded, an audience
gathers in every void.
But I want no stories or poems

only your voice among
the bric-a-brac
of the warm ruins where we make our home,
saying nothing.

STANCE

I have applied to go
beyond the supple wall
which is the moment,
a wall built of flowerdust
and the smell of water.

Is it possible to lie prone
without the feet balancing
past and forward?

Ah, the questions of the day;
they will fade as we concede
monopoly to the tenses.
One says the ordinary thing
but with the wrong gesture.

THE REASK

This is a bare room,
an area for a time
walled off, removed
from direct day
so that it depends
outwards for light,
empty of self but for its shell.

Even at the darkest
moment of night
the body still glows
brighter than this
as the window glows
with the faint sky
feeding the nightsoul.

Morning comes to the still lane
hooped with blind roses,
spotted with haws.
The sun falls aslant
the laneway like a golden
swath of corn. I reap tares
inside the Reask, lying alone.

Day burns its slow wick down.
The earth warms and turns away.
The sun moves the distant sunflowers:
their flesh is soft bread steaming.
With dusk they drop their heads
like young lovers
disappointed but faithful.

°WAKING
in memory of my father, died November 1960

Someone is breathing in the room
apart from me. It is my father;
I recognise the hiss of his nostrils
closing, closing. . . . It is late;
he is doing Milltown work,
we can use the extra money.
That stub in his hand is a rent book
high as a bible, thin as his widow.
Below it, in the shadow, I imagine
the soft metal of his heart
(a gold cog, slipping) finally burred,
refusing to bite. For my life
I cannot picture him; details
melt into light. The angle
of his nose, the slight furrow
of moustache escape me. All I have
is that sound fathered in darkness
carrying a reek of tobacco-y linen,
the taste of his lip.
                    He rustles
like a curtain. Outside it is six a.m.
A sudden fleet of cars passes
drowning my breath for about the length
of a funeral. This has gone on ten years.

THE DREAM UP

Coming to a perpendicular bank
I am face to face with my only escape;
it is a <u>liana,</u> it is an artery
thick and smooth as a wooden rope
quivering in the surface of the clay.

I begin climbing up the long beam
hand over hand turning with the handle.
Nearing the top I am breathless,
spittle and tongue flecked with detritus.
My feet weigh nine stone each over the drop.

Grappling for the final manoeuvre
I see that the beam has been a scythe
plunged into the edge of the drop, blade down.
Searching for the upper metal my fingers slice.

At last I pull myself upright;
I have come up out of my quarry.
Standing on the plateau blood drips
from my hands on to the green grass.

THE TRIAL

With all those children
ranked on the staircase
like an advertisement
for Fry's cocoa

he still managed music
in the wooden loft,
the floor dry as cornflour,
Frau B waiting for her song-book.

His feet on the pedals
clacked like butter bats;
ratchets and keys
flew invisibly

past a sexton wheezing
at the end of an air pump.
The racket filled
the whole gallery.

Night trooped into the pews,
a congregation dressed
exclusively in black,
an audience of air.

Unaware of the German
landscape all about him;
a pigeon settled on the ridge tile,
and he heard a book closing.

Refugees straggling south
found no light but paused.
Down in the chancel
a solitary prayer

waited listening, unanswered.
Each note matched with another
chosen after a long courtship.
All were now paired like raised hands;

noise receded and the bills paid.
When he rose with a sigh
from the manuals (the pigeon
asleep and the boards velvet)

the sound of clapping
startled him till he saw
a figure waiting below
where the music had fallen.

Beckoning with weary relief
he made him welcome
and led the way in
towards the crowded benches.

MASTRIM: A MEDITATION

I

We who heard the lonely call
found consolation in the hall;

those inside around the board
learned to miss the bated word

they used themselves about the house,
afraid to pick the wild rose.

The place grew silent when they spoke
as if their voices might evoke

impressions on the useless bed
beneath the streaming windowhead.

We served remotely at the call
as if waiters bearing offal

for days had stood attentive; night
found us weeping at the right

of their shrill neglect of us,
now banished to outoffices

from where at last we saw the beams
float downwards burning through their dream.

We walk towards a field, but grass
has turned to fire as we pass,

and every value of the grange
has altered with us, yet is strange.

A world which lies beyond our sense
invades with hostile innocence.

We are unborn, discarded myth
walking in the field of truth.

II

A halt in the desert where I have in mind
a garden in Russia, ringed by bright earth.
The air lies thickly in the boughs of trees.
The mole rests below, heartshaped and blind,
in his darker element. The birds walk
through the thorns, unmolested by my noise.
I am nothing now but the seer of
moonlight falling like a stick of chalk.

When Maria came here in June, the roses
were drest in snow, and the one-wheeled phaeton
had not turned on the road to Granard
at flung roadmetal under the willows;
no urchin hedgehog sinned in the gravel.
Westward to the dark sea the diocese
lay waiting for the rootless freedom tree
and the planters' shout again 'hang the Devil'.

And it was warm and still enough for snow.
We ran like dogs through the generations
tonguing the scent that our own game trailed,
writing on windows and fields one word Now.

Bold John, riding from Shelton to Ticknock
to eat well and to take rents at Mastrim,
rises stiff-faced and hale in the morning,
his excrement smelling of woodcock.

Behind the hedge the ladies play tennis,
a globe passing between two tensions.
The unseen has become their dimension
as they keep within their painted limits.
A buried box in the garden saved us,
an infant buried safely till midnight
during disaffection when we shook
at the promise of our best ambitions.

Then the gate grudged over the humped pathway,
a contralto warning of our encroachment
into a world where the blood crackled
and shivered, weakly rhyming in the clay.
Soon the shadows bloomed in the furniture;
the carpet breathed its own life into ours.
In the evening the house hummed with birdsong
and the empty shelves did not fail to answer.

We said that we were the first born outside
the garden though our eyes were shaped like flowers.
The dressed stone of our facade was foreign
to the coast, silkbeautiful, silkfragile.
After that failure we have never stirred
from the room, stare across the area
at the latticed countryside, raised hands
and neutral voices, seen and never heard.

III

'The window makes the hills a picture.'
And we gaze tiredly at the loughside,
the whole amphitheatre stuffed with air,
even among the shingle and between
the curved and ageing stems of a foot-high lawn.
The cistern sighs in the toilet upstairs.
Wings of the candleflame are swarming.
An influence from the window shuffles
the papers; the level of whiskey
stumbles in the bottle, and air tops it up.
There is time to be lost, and to regain
the things which make history, and not time.

Tomorrow I'll struggle with this vision
like vomiting on an empty stomach.

IV

Darkness also reaches towards noon,
where he lies stunned by the heating system,
and birds at the window sing in Greek.
A rich disaster of the moment.

He will remember nonsense
of what passed, and little of that.
The kettle calling to the pot
'anything, anything you like.'

V

I heard a slaughter on the lawn,
the noise of sleeping from the bawn.

And through a limbo of the air
my simple soul could never dare

to stop the leaf from falling in
the mulch of human carrion.

I heard what the convolvulus
bugled in its tiny voice,

a note not deeper than the blade
which rested in my wooden blood.

Nobody stepped from the demesne
to rescue either from his pain;

a gasp of pleasure from the lodge
shuddered the remaining hedge.

VI *Abides*

Standing by doorways and looking inwards as if to keep
    watch near the open window, listening to the slates
    as they cool and to other sounds, our own stillness.
    Under myopic ceilings in other rooms and mo-
    ments when our bones contract the faces we see
    are savage, learned.

By the fallen bough are iron shards of a bowl the children drank from, a closed well, a bangle of weeds. The orchard turns round the lost woman standing in colourless muslin, her eyes speeding. Grass springs upright underneath her.

What has waited for light to climb the hedge, for the green moss on appletrees to blench? If the adder and the vixen have never eaten here, can the garden be empty yet? We hear no pigeons grunting nor the bat choking on insect juice. Trouping to a previous request we make no impression on the place, din or dint of foot. It should destroy us now to see her tears.

But in open country the wind sounds stiller, cornering on the bone-less part of the ear, in the hair naturally, and on the further limbs.

Echoes are solely heard in an empty home, movements of sound against an abiding vacuum. Not a breath shakes the paper ferns.

Though there were wooden bread and fishes in the mantel, we remember the clap-clap of the electric waterpump, and the false distinctions of linoleum tiles. Birds in a garden know that the dark is old. They are nameless and singing.

ELEGIES

I

When John Donne dropped to sleep all around him slept.
Pictures were drowsy on the wall, the floor
was deep in rugs and tables; furniture
whose certain essence was a sleep that kept
the clocks as motionless as lumber.
At rest in cupboards as in dormitories
the linen slept as though it were bodies
draped in animal slumber.
Night was not idly here and there
turning the key or coiled in locks
but paused in heat exhaling human shocks
to be at once impenetrable as air.
All slept: the window in its envelope
of snow might never have been written;
the words it might have read remained unseen
when John Donne unwakened and took his sleep.

The iron weights in the butcher's shop are prone
in care of watchdogs shrunken from the chains.
Mice are asleep and cats stiffened; the Thames
nods its way towards a salted dawn
shaking the reflected tower and arch.
Ships are anchorless by the wharf safely.
The sea lies down beside a promontory,
the land her bolster, intent and white as starch.
The walls of the gaol loosen in this rest
and prisoners lie still in their freedom
heedless of a momentary calm
before light draws its finger from the east.

The angels also sleep above the globe,
a world forgotten by the sleeping saints.
In holy shame fair paradise faints
under the waves of the Lord's deepest robe.
Gehenna sleeps and man must fail to be;
John Donne fails to-night his last disaster;
his breath and kiss and manly lines are lost.
Satan sleeps, and with him all enmity.
The prophets sleep. Good rests on Evil's arm.
The paling snow completes its last full stop
as his stressed and weary syllables drop
in place, to his drift of words' alarm.
Everybody sleeps: the saints, devils, God,
friends, deceitful servants, lovers in bed
lie dormant on this night John Donne is dead.
And the snow shuffles its feet on the road.

II

In the darkness of the white snowroad
I hear a cry, I hear a frightened call
as if a man were left to carry all
the bitter climate with his own painful load.
He is weeping. Yes, somebody is there,
his voice flaking at the brink of silence
like nervous hands, thin as a needle's
eye and blind of thread. Somebody is near.
Whose tears are these that I hear in darkness?
An angel, waiting in a cape of snow
for re-birth of my last-year's love below?
Oh, seraph, do I recognise your voice?

I have often heard them in sombre course.
Have you absconded from my sleeping church

to troop in silence under this dark birch,
or have your vain trumpetings made you hoarse?

Then, Paul, this silence canvasses your name,
the darkness surely being pure as glass.
And yet your voice was distinctly harsh
from straight talk, driving the pegs of Christ's claim.
Or, is our Father here, whose mighty hand
has loomed over this place time out of mind?
'Speak, Lord, thy servant heareth.' Oh I find
the impress of Thy silence stuns the land.
Was I alone to keep my open eyes
when guardsmen gathered in impassive gloom?
Gabriel! announce your presence, whom
I knew to summon myriads in the skies.

'No, it is I your soul, John Donne, complains;
alone on heaven's pinnacle I weep
for things my labour, even at its neap,
had set afloat, thoughts heavy as chains.
You were aloft, and from the heights you saw
a people whole. Despite your load you could
fly again through sin and passion to God;
Hell having seen, first as image, then raw.
Seeing life, your *Island* was its twin.
And soaring past your lord, in pride fell
content with burdens in the abysmal
tide of the roaring ocean.
From then the Lord seemed but a light that gleams
and all His Radiant Country was to you
a fitful image moving to and fro —
marsh-fire, a credal squint, or just a dream.
His fields persist unbroken by a plough;
the years lie fallow and the eras;

rain dances hugely in the formal grass;
a perfect tense preserves your broken vow.
But here I stand and weep; the road is gone.
I cannot fly with my spirit's temple
before death brings to me his ample
deductions and certainty of tone.
I languish in a passion of desire
stitching the last remnant of my spirit,
the needle passing through my soul in merit
of the empty snow so uselessly pure.

'But listen! while my weeping now disturbs
your rest, the busy snow shuttles through the dark
unmelting but sewing up our hurt.
Endlessly to and fro the needle works.
It is not I who weep but you, John Donne;
who lies alone. Your poems in presses sleep
while snow assumes your house into the deep
and snow is drifting down from darkest Heaven.'

III

All things are sunk in sleep. The final verse
awaits its cue baring its teeth to snarl
that earthly love is just a joker's role
and heavenly love becomes a friar's flesh.
We find in life companions of such pith
that life is shared and ground to common salt;
but there's no lover under Heaven's vault
can intimate our soul and share our death.
Man's coat is tattered. And it may be torn
by all who want to tear it more.
It frays and is redeemed to soar
briefly, the wearer's shroud. Once more it's worn.

Sleep soundly, Donne, and let your soul not mope
in such dejected rags as darkness gives.
The convex sky is glowing like a sieve
and holy stars invest your world with Hope.

NOTES

'DOWTH'

The least of the three great tumuli of the Boyne Valley has been vandalised throughout the centuries, but the pleasure dome of an eighteenth-century landlord has disappeared from the top of the mound.

'RISK'

Máirtín Ó Cadhain, the outstanding writer of fiction in modern Irish, was professor of Irish in Dublin University (Trinity College) for a few years before his death in 1970. *The Sheaves are Stacked* (an approximate translation) was his last collection of stories.

'MASTRIM: A MEDITATION'

Mastrim was the original name of the area developed by the Edgeworths in the northern midlands of Ireland.

'ELEGIES'

The poem, though it is a good deal shorter than the original, is based on Josef Brodsky's *Elegy for John Donne*. My thanks to Neil Cornwell for supplying me with a literal translation of the Russian text, and for remaining silent about the liberties I have taken.

ACKNOWLEDGEMENTS

Some of these poems, or versions of them, first appeared in *Atlantis, Cyphers, The Irish Press, Irish University Review, The Malahat Review,* and *The Sphere Book of Modern Irish Poetry;* to the editors acknowledgement is duly made for permission to publish them here. Two poems from an earlier period, and now much amended, have been included.